NIGHTWALKER'S SONG

Johann Wolfgang von
Goethe

Translated & introduced by
John Greening

2022

Published by Arc Publications,
Nanholme Mill, Shaw Wood Road
Todmorden OL14 6DA, UK
www.arcpublications.co.uk

Translation copyright © John Greening, 2022
Introduction copyright © John Greening, 2022
Copyright in the present edition © Arc Publications 2022

978 1911469 25 4

Design by Tony Ward
Printed in the UK by TJ Books Limited.

Cover photograph:
'Schwarzwald' (1986) by Jane Greening

The frontispiece is a reproduction of
'Wandrers Nachtlied' (Nightwalker's Song) written
in Goethe's own hand on the wall of a hunter's cabin – later
known as *Goethehäuschen* (Goethe's cabin) –
on the Kickelhahn mountain in Ilmenau, Thuringia,
during the night 6 / 7 September 1780.

Acknowledgements
The translator would like thank Jean Boase-Beier
for her invaluable help and advice in the
preparation of this chapbook.

This book is in copyright. Subject to statutory exception and
to provision of relevant collective licensing agreements, no
reproduction of any part of this book may take place without
the written permission of Arc Publications.

Arc Chapbook Series
Series Editor: Tony Ward

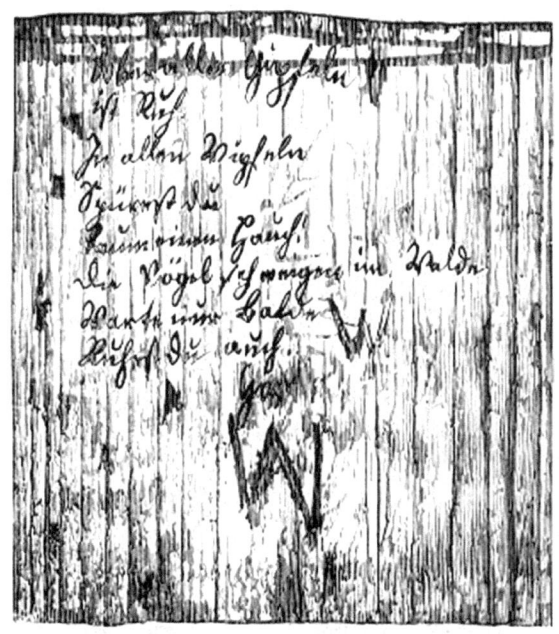

Goethe's Handschrift im Kickelhahn-Häuschen.

CONTENTS

Introduction / 6

10 / Wandrers Nachtlied • Nightwalker's Song / 11

10 / Willkommen und Abschied • Welcome and Farewell / 11

14 / Prometheus • Prometheus / 15

18 / Harzreise im Winter • Harz Mountains, Winter Journey / 19

24 / Römische Elegien • Roman Elegies / 25

28 / Nähe des Geliebten • Her Nearness / 29

30 / Der Zauberlehrling • The Sorcerer's Apprentice / 31

36 / Faust im Studierzimmer • Faust in his Study / 37

42 / Natur und Kunst • Nature and Art / 43

Biographical Notes / 44

INTRODUCTION

The full scope of Goethe's genius is best conveyed in G. H. Lewes's immensely readable English biography,[1] published not long after the poet's death. Since he regarded his entire output as 'fragments of one great confession', it's not unreasonable to encourage newcomers to begin with such a 'Life'.[2] Goethe was born at a time when rationalist 'Enlightenment' philosophies were being unsettled by the random horror of the Lisbon earthquake. If it was an age more suited to a Pope than a Coleridge, there were elements of both in Johann Wolfgang. The first poems came early – even some lines in English when he was sixteen – and his style proceeded to develop and flourish as vigorously as any of the plants he would later study: from the first rococo idylls, love poems and occult dabblings, the back-to-nature lyrical ballads and free verse 'hymns' to the classical (but very modern-sounding) *Roman Elegies* and *Venetian Epigrams*, the epic, *Hermann and Dorothea* and the astonishingly liberated *West-Eastern Divan*, as high-spirited a work of old age as anything W. B. Yeats managed.

Beyond the biographical facts, however, Goethe is a difficult poet to place, not least because he lived so long. As a child he heard Mozart perform; as a man he knew both Beethoven and Mendelssohn. Yeats is in fact quite a good equivalent. Both poets changed as the world changed, not to mention their parallel engagement with a national theatre and shared passion for the occult. There were indeed many different stages to Goethe's development and he had practical and scientific expertise in an extraordinary number of areas (here he leaves WBY in the dust).

All this may explain a certain wariness towards him in England, where Thomas Carlyle's 'universal man' can be all too easily characterised as a Jack-of-all-trades.

[1] Lewes, George Henry, *The Life and Works of Goethe* (1855).
[2] Or even with my little biographical summary on p. 44.

While well-educated German families have long been expected to 'devote at least a yard of book-shelving to him' (as Ronald Gray puts it in *Goethe: a Critical Introduction*, 1967), to many in English-speaking countries Goethe is merely an unpronounceable name: alluded to, but little read, his handsome features unlikely to be on a modern student's smartphone. Any enthusiasm has been reserved for his play *Faust* (and then only for Part I; Lewes called Part II 'an elaborate mistake') although it is rarely staged in Britain – compared for example with the number of Shakespeare productions in Germany, where one might almost think it was he who was born in Frankfurt. Nevertheless, several poets over the years have tried translating his most famous play into English. Coleridge's version particularly interested Goethe (who never made it to England) but it is Louis MacNeice's translation that most readers will know. Randall Jarrell's is good (his widow remarked, somewhat to this translator's relief, that Jarrell didn't speak German – 'mostly because he wouldn't'), although David Constantine's is probably the best for the 2020s. Constantine, Michael Hamburger and Christopher Middleton apart, contemporary English poets have largely ignored the poetry. Even T. S. Eliot barely mentions it in his landmark essay, *Goethe as the Sage*. Nor will readers often stumble on individual translations of Goethe as they might find a Rilke or a Hölderlin as part of a modern poet's latest slim volume.

It's true that there is a bewildering amount of Goethe poetry, yet the poems are in many ways the best introduction – much more engaging than the often undramatic dramas or the novels. *Elective Affinities* is a mildly engaging piece of artifice, *The Sorrows of Young Werther* hard going, for all the excitement when it appeared in 1774 (the only modern equivalent would be Beatlemania or the Harry Potter phenomenon, except that this involved copycat suicides, much to Goethe's discomfort). Similar reservations might strike anyone reading some of the early verses, but my hope is that this tightly-focused selection will show why Goethe is more than a historical polymath and how his poems can still have a powerful impact. One touchstone for me was 'Harzreise im Winter', not least because it's in free verse. It would be good to encounter this poem as often as one finds modern versions of, say, Rilke's 'First Duino Elegy'. I hope my efforts might encourage fellow poets to try. We need multiple translations: the aim is to stir some awareness and interest.

My own interest and awareness were shamefully slow. At university in Swansea in 1972, I bought a Penguin edition of the poetry with David Luke's prose translations. It didn't make much impression, but I persevered during a postgraduate year in Mannheim, where I was allegedly studying verse drama, though mostly idling in the concert hall. Nevertheless my love of music meant that I knew Schubert's song settings, the extracts from *Faust* in Mahler's Eighth, Schumann's curious three-part oratorio *Scenes from Goethe's Faust*, and what Berlioz, Gounod, Liszt had made of him.[3] I remember trying to appreciate his range, buying cheap East German editions, even taking the tram to Heidelberg on successive nights to see a rare production of the complete *Faust II*. But my knowledge remained fragmentary, my understanding poor, so I set him aside for half a century.

It was only during the recent pandemic that I returned to Goethe in versions by Christopher Middleton. Although Middleton is a fine poet whose understanding of German is in a different league from mine, I felt that his mixing of contemporary and archaic registers didn't quite work. Looking for alternatives, I found that the few who had translated him simply weren't natural poets, and those

---

[3] Hector Berlioz's "légende dramatique" *La damnation de Faust* was first performed at the Opéra-Comique in Paris on 6 December 1846; Charles Gounod's opera *Faust* was premiered in 1859 in Paris; and the first performance of Franz Liszt's choral symphony *The Faust Symphony* took place in Weimar on 5 September 1857, for the inauguration of the Goethe–Schiller Monument there.

who were (like Vernon Watkins) often ran into tonal difficulties. Even Michael Hamburger's English verse could be rather bloodless. So I began to experiment, using cribs and dictionaries to guide my understanding, but aiming to create musically satisfying English poems. While these are hardly Lowellesque 'imitations' I wanted them to have a contemporary texture. I didn't hesitate to convert or even modernise an image or an idea if it helped the poem adapt to a different age and culture. I have shadowed Goethe's original metres – counting stresses rather than syllables – and retained rhyme schemes, sometimes adapting, or using pararhyme and internal rhyme. I particularly wanted to catch the outrageous playfulness of 'The Sorcerer's Apprentice', hearing Goethe's music for once, rather than Paul Dukas's. Readers who know the film *Fantasia* may be surprised to discover how closely Mickey Mouse's antics follow those of the original 'Zauberlehrling'.

My selections are mostly from the earlier part of Goethe's long creative life: poems or extracts from poems to which I felt I could do justice, along with some that everyone ought to know – including German literature's most famous and famously hard-to-translate eight lines: 'Wandrers Nachtlied' (German translators of 'I wandered lonely as a cloud' have it easy in comparison). Here are lyric poem, love poem, conversation poem, travel poem, elegy, epigram, satire, sonnet, song, ballad, comic narrative, erotic confessional, dramatic monologue. Even such a tiny portion of Goethe's vast output can, I think, give some idea of the man's versatility, the variety of voice and preoccupation. For those who wish to explore further, there is David Luke's newly versified edition of the poems,[4] and I'd also recommend Jeremy Adler's brief critical introduction, *Johann Wolfgang von Goethe*, although the most thorough and entertaining book about him remains Lewes's *The Life and Works of Goethe*.

[4] *Johann Wolfgang von Goethe: Selected Poetry* trans. David Luke (Penguin, 2005).

WANDRERS NACHTLIED

Über allen Gipfeln
Ist Ruh,
In allen Wipfeln
Spürest du
Kaum einen Hauch;
Die Vögelein schweigen im Walde.
Warte nur, balde
Ruhest du auch.

WILLKOMMEN UND ABSCHIED

Es schlug mein Herz, geschwind, zu Pferde!
Es war getan fast eh gedacht.
Der Abend wiegte schon die Erde,
Und an den Bergen hing die Nacht;
Schon stand im Nebelkleid die Eiche,
Ein aufgetürmter Riese, da,
Wo Finsternis aus dem Gesträuche
Mit hundert schwarzen Augen sah.

NIGHTWALKER'S SONG

> *Goethe's most celebrated lyric was composed in September 1780 on Kickelhahn mountain near Ilmenau after he had visited a mine with his friend, patron and employer, Karl August, Duke of Saxe-Weimar-Eisenach. He inscribed the text on the wall of a hunting lodge he was staying in. Years later (the day before his 82nd birthday) he returned to see the pencil inscription beside the south window. It is a poem in which sound is crucial; the line breaks are as vital as the words.*

A calmness hanging over
the peaks:
the trees not even
breathing, none
speaks a word to you.
The birds are quiet in the forest.
Rest here, and soon
you'll be calmer too.

WELCOME AND FAREWELL

> *One of the best known early poems (Schubert set it), written when Goethe was in love with Friederike Brion. As Christopher Middleton says: 'the verse is formal, but the tempi are quick, emotions violent and volatile'. My version favours pararhyme, which if not quite modern dress at least removes the wig and whiskers.*

My heart beat. On my horse, away,
as if the thought itself had spurs.
The earth joined evening where she lay
and night hung on the rugged moors;
around one giant oak a curl
of mist was clinging; from the haze
in banks and hedgerows you could feel
a hundred small black beady eyes.

Der Mond von einem Wolkenhügel
Sah kläglich aus dem Duft hervor,
Die Winde schwangen leise Flügel,
Umsausten schauerlich mein Ohr;
Die Nacht schuf tausend Ungeheuer,
Doch frisch und fröhlich war mein Mut:
In meinen Adern welches Feuer!
In meinem Herzen welche Glut!

Dich sah ich, und die milde Freude
Floß von dem süßen Blick auf mich;
Ganz war mein Herz an deiner Seite
Und jeder Atemzug für dich.
Ein rosenfarbnes Frühlingswetter
Umgab das liebliche Gesicht,
Und Zärtlichkeit für mich – ihr Götter!
Ich hofft es, ich verdient es nicht!

Doch ach, schon mit der Morgensonne
Verengt der Abschied mir das Herz:
In deinen Küssen welche Wonne!
In deinem Auge welcher Schmerz!
Ich ging, du standst und sahst zur Erden,
Und sahst mir nach mit nassem Blick:
Und doch, welch Glück, geliebt zu werden!
Und lieben, Götter, welch ein Glück!

The moon looked sadly through a veil
of cloud, the winds began to beat
soft whirring wings about me, till
my ears could bear no more; the night
revealed its thousand horror masks.
And yet my fiery spirits cheered,
hotly defying such grotesques,
from heart and veins the lava poured.

I saw you, and that gentle calm
flowed from your glance and out to me.
As soon as you approached, I came
alive in every breath. The way
that rosy spring-like morning glow
intensified your lovely face,
that tenderness towards me – how
I'd dreamt of (not deserved) all this.

But once the sun had risen, that's
when parting had its painful say.
Your kisses took me to the heights,
your eyes the depths of misery.
I left; you just looked down, or gave
the briefest glance, through mounting tears.
And yet, to have been loved – to love,
ye gods, such utter happiness.

PROMETHEUS

Bedecke deinen Himmel, Zeus,
Mit Wolkendunst
Und übe, dem Knaben gleich,
Der Disteln köpft
An Eichen dich und Bergeshöhn;
Mußt mir meine Erde
Doch lassen stehen
Und meine Hütte die du nicht gebaut,
Und meinen Herd,
Um dessen Glut
Du mich beneidest.

Ich kenne nichts Ärmeres
Unter der Sonn als euch, Götter!
Ihr nähret kümmerlich
Von Opfersteuern
Und Gebetshauch
Eure Majestät
Und darbtet, wären
Nicht Kinder und Bettler
Hoffnungsvolle Toren.

Da ich ein Kind war,
Nicht wußte, wo aus noch ein,
Kehrt ich mein verirrtes Auge
Zur Sonne, als wenn drüber wär
Ein Ohr, zu hören meine Klage,
Ein Herz wie meins,
Sich des Bedrängten zu erbarmen.

PROMETHEUS

> Composed in Goethe's early twenties, but published in 1789, this dramatic monologue is characteristic of the 'Sturm und Drang' era. It is from an uncompleted play about the Titan who stole fire from the gods to give to man and was chained to a rock where his liver was pecked out each day. Goethe sympathised – as a young poet, he 'had to exclude all aid from men... I separated myself from the gods also'. Prometheus's heroism certainly appealed to the emerging scientist in him.

Make sure you're safe up there
behind cloud cover, Zeus,
keeping your eye in (like a boy
who grabs at thistleheads)
by targeting oak and peak.
Earth you'd better leave
unharmed at least, and
my shed, which you didn't build,
with its inefficient heater,
whose self-sufficient flame
you seem to envy me.

Nothing under the sun is
as desperately poor as you are,
you gods, force-feeding
your glory with husks
of prayer-breath and let
blood, and you would
starve if it weren't for
their idiotic optimism –
the wretched and the young.

When I was a child and un-
attuned to what is what,
I turned my misdirected gaze
on the sun as if it were
a counsellor, some fellow
sufferer, ready to warm
those icy pressures within me.

Wer half mir
Wider der Titanen Übermut?
Wer rettete vom Tode mich,
Von Sklaverei?
Hast du nicht alles selbst vollendet,
Heilig glühend Herz?
Und glühtest jung und gut,
Betrogen, Rettungsdank
Dem Schlafenden da droben?

Ich dich ehren? Wofür?
Hast du die Schmerzen gelindert
Je des Beladenen?
Hast du die Tränen gestillet
Je des Geängsteten?
Hat nicht mich zum Manne geschmiedet
Die allmächtige Zeit
Und das ewige Schicksal,
Meine Herrn und deine?

Wähntest du etwa,
Ich sollte das Leben hassen,
In Wüsten fliehen,
Weil nicht alle
Blütenträume reiften?

Hier sitz ich, forme Menschen
Nach meinem Bilde,
Ein Geschlecht, das mir gleich sei,
Zu leiden, zu weinen,
Zu genießen und zu freuen sich
Und dein nicht zu achten,
Wie ich!

Who helped me
stand up to the Titans and their hubris?
Who snatched me from a likely death
or certain slavery?
Wasn't it you, heart of mine,
who did this all yourself,
sacred, ablaze, and glowing youthful cheerful
mistaken gratitude
towards that lofty snoring?

Honour you? For what?
Have you ever offered to lift
this agony that presses
on me or done the slightest
to ease my daily meltdowns?
Was I not beaten into a man
by the fist of Chairman Time
and the indefatigability
of Fate, who commands us both?

Did you just assume that I
would end up hating life
and take off into no man's land
when I found that none of my
dreams had come to fruition?

I sit here, manufacturing
bodies in my own image,
a new range programmed
to suffer and to weep,
or whoop and punch the air –
but who, like me, won't care
about you.

HARZREISE IM WINTER

Dem Geier gleich,
Der auf schweren Morgenwolken
Mit sanftem Fittich ruhend
Nach Beute schaut,
Schwebe mein Lied.

Denn ein Gott hat
Jedem seine Bahn
Vorgezeichnet,
Die der Glückliche
Rasch zum freudigen
Ziele rennt:
Wem aber Unglück
Das Herz zusammenzog,
Er sträubt vergebens
Sich gegen die Schranken
Des ehernen Fadens,
Den die doch bittre Schere
Nur einmal löst.

In Dickichts-Schauer
Drängt sich das rauhe Wild,
Und mit den Sperlingen
Haben längst die Reichen
In ihre Sümpfe sich gesenkt.

HARZ MOUNTAINS, WINTER JOURNEY

One of Goethe's many poems about destiny (used by Brahms in his Alto Rhapsody), it is surprisingly modern-sounding: he might almost have been prompted by Robert Lowell to 'say what happened'. If free verse was a surprising departure, so was the trip itself, although he was ostensibly prospecting for minerals on behalf of the Duke, and this may even have been composed on horseback. Goethe's real purpose that winter of 1777 was to climb the Brocken, which he did in dreadful conditions (and partly in homage to Petrarch). The experience is recreated at the end of the poem.

Like a red kite
against the weight of morning cloud,
its wings barely stirring
as it scans for prey,
may this hover...

After all, it is a god
has designated
each of us a path,
which the luckier
rush along towards
their happy ending:
but those whose spirits
misfortune has
broken, struggle
in vain against the limits
permitted by that fibre
the shears cut
once, and bitterly.

Into thickest gloom
a wild boar plunges,
the wealthy already snug
on their floodplains
like so many sparrows.

Leicht ists folgen dem Wagen,
Den Fortuna führt,
Wie der gemächliche Troß
Auf gebesserten Wegen
Hinter des Fürsten Einzug.

Aber abseits wer ists?
Ins Gebüsch verliert sich sein Pfad,
Hinter ihm schlagen
Die Sträuche zusammen,
Das Gras steht wieder auf,
Die Öde verschlingt ihn.

Ach, wer heilet die Schmerzen
Des, dem Balsam zu Gift ward?
Der sich Menschenhaß
Aus der Fülle der Liebe trank?
Erst verachtet, nun ein Verächter,
Zehrt er heimlich auf
Seinen eignen Wert
In ungnügender Selbstsucht.

Ist auf deinem Psalter,
Vater der Liebe, ein Ton
Seinem Ohre vernehmlich,
So erquicke sein Herz!
Öffne den umwölkten Blick
Über die tausend Quellen
Neben dem Durstenden
In der Wüste.

Der du der Freuden viel schaffst,
Jedem ein überfließend Maß,
Segne die Brüder der Jagd
Auf der Fährte des Wilds
Mit jugendlichem Übermut
Fröhlicher Mordsucht,

Easy enough to track
the progress of fortune:
follow where the sleek
motorcade takes you,
up those spruced boulevards.

But who's that winking on to
the slip-road, fading into
a verge that blurs his lights,
cow parsley springing back
as he's claimed by edgelands?

Tell me the cure for someone
poisoned by their own linctus,
who imbibed misanthropy
even as they poured out love?
The mocker-in-chief mocked
and quietly gnawing on
his own personal goodness,
always hungry for more.

Father of Love, is there
a tune that might get through
to him in your hymn book?
Revive that old original,
prise open those clouds
shrouding his parched view
of the thousand springs
around him in the desert?

You who have given us
different kinds of pleasure,
guide my fellow hunters
on the scent of whatever
their youthful energy
and cheerful bloodlust

Späte Rächer des Unbills,
Dem schon Jahre vergeblich
Wehrt mit Knütteln der Bauer.

Aber den Einsamen hüll
In deine Goldwolken!
Umgib mit Wintergrün,
Bis die Rose wieder heranreift,
Die feuchten Haare,
O Liebe, deines Dichters!

Mit der dämmernden Fackel
Leuchtest du ihm
Durch die Furten bei Nacht,
Über grundlose Wege
Auf öden Gefilden;
Mit dem tausendfarbigen Morgen
Lachst du ins Herz ihm;
Mit dem beizenden Sturm
Trägst du ihn hoch empor;
Winterströme stürzen vom Felsen
In seine Psalmen,
Und Altar des lieblichsten Danks
Wird ihm des gefürchteten Gipfels
Schneebehangner Scheitel,
Den mit Geisterreihen
Kränzten ahnende Völker.

Du stehst mit unerforschtem Busen
Geheimnisvoll offenbar
Über der erstaunten Welt
Und schaust aus Wolken
Auf ihre Reiche und Herrlichkeit,
Die du aus den Adern deiner Brüder
Neben dir wässerst.

desire, final nemesis of
all that the cultivators
have been battling for years.

But wrap the loner
in your golden cloud
and with the green
of winter, with love, wire
your poet's soaking hair
until the rose returns.

Light him by the
flicker of your screen
through night's fords,
its crumbling cliffs
and disused airfields.
Raise him a multi-coloured
smile with the dawn.
Raise the highest pitch
of storm thrill for him.
Let the winter ghylls
cascade into his singing,
and your dreaded peak
become his grateful altar,
that snow-covered scalp
reeling with spirits
bestowed on it by folklore.

You keep your secrets close,
yet bare yourself
above the astonished world,
and witness from the clouds
its privilege, its power,
which you nourish from the veins
of those most near to you.

RÖMISCHE ELEGIEN

I

Saget, Steine, mir an, o sprecht, ihr hohen Paläste!
    Straßen, redet ein Wort! Genius, regst du dich nicht?
Ja, es ist alles beseelt in deinen heiligen Mauern,
    Ewige Roma; nur mir schweiget noch alles so still.
O wer flüstert mir zu, an welchem Fenster erblick ich
    Einst das holde Geschöpf, das mich versengend erquickt?
Ahn ich die Wege noch nicht, durch die ich immer und immer,
    Zu ihr und von ihr zu gehn, opfre die köstliche Zeit?
Noch betracht ich Kirch und Palast, Ruinen und Säulen,
    Wie ein bedächtiger Mann schicklich die Reise benutzt.
Doch bald ist es vorbei; dann wird ein einziger Tempel,
    Amors Tempel, nur sein, der den Geweihten empfängt.
Eine Welt zwar bist du, o Rom; doch ohne die Liebe
    Wäre die Welt nicht die Welt, wäre denn Rom auch nicht Rom.

V

Froh empfind ich mich nun auf klassischem Boden begeistert;
    Vor- und Mitwelt spricht lauter und reizender mir.
Hier befolg ich den Rat, durchblättre die Werke der Alten
    Mit geschäftiger Hand, täglich mit neuem Genuß.
Aber die Nächte hindurch hält Amor mich anders beschäftigt;
    Werd ich auch halb nur gelehrt, bin ich doch doppelt beglückt.
Und belehr ich mich nicht, wenn ich des lieblichen Busens
    Formen spähe, die Hand leite die Hüften hinab?

ROMAN ELEGIES

These products of Goethe's travels in Italy (1786-88) reflect his reading of classical poets yet can sound like late Auden: conversational, opinionated. G. H. Lewes called them 'the most perfect poems of the kind in all literature', entitling Goethe to 'first place among German poets'. There are twenty elegiac couplets – elegies in the sense Donne used for his love poems. The woman behind most of them is Christiane Vulpius, whom he met on his return.

I

Say something, stones! Reply, you looming palaces!
    Nothing from the streets? Will 'the Glory that was Rome'
not stir? Oh, there's life enough to be found
    within your holy precincts, it's simply ignoring me.
Surely someone will hiss for my attention and point to
    that window where she'll be, who both singes and enlivens?
Don't I know too well the roads I've been fated to take
    towards her and back from her, scattering precious time?
I'm peering at church and palace, ruin and column still,
    like a sobersides who uses his annual vacation wisely.
But soon that will be over, and just the single temple
    devoted to love will remain to excite the devotee.
It's true you're a world in yourself, Rome, but lacking love
    this world would be no world; nor would Rome be Rome.

V

Inspiring to find myself once again on classical ground,
    where past and present both speak with a stronger appeal.
I've followed advice and am spending more time with the Ancients,
    leafing busily through their Collected Works for pleasure,
by day – by night, a different pleasure, and oh I'm busy,
    half the scholar, but twice as happy. Anyway, isn't
this learning of a kind, to study the contours of her breasts
    or let my hands explore the country around her hips?

Dann versteh ich den Marmor erst recht: ich denk und vergleiche,
  Sehe mit fühlendem Aug, fühle mit sehender Hand.
Raubt die Liebste denn gleich mir einige Stunden des Tages,
  Gibt sie Stunden der Nacht mir zur Entschädigung hin.
Wird doch nicht immer geküßt, es wird vernünftig gesprochen;
  Überfällt sie der Schlaf, lieg ich und denke mir viel.
Oftmals hab ich auch schon in ihren Armen gedichtet
  Und des Hexameters Maß leise mit fingernder Hand
Ihr auf den Rücken gezählt. Sie atmet in lieblichem Schlummer,
  Und es durchglühet ihr Hauch mir bis ins Tiefste die Brust.
Amor schüret die Lamp indes und denket der Zeiten,
  Da er den nämlichen Dienst seinen Triumvirn getan.

XIV

Zünde mir Licht an, Knabe – «Noch ist es hell. Ihr verzehret
  Öl und Docht nur umsonst. Schließet die Läden doch nicht!
Hinter die Häuser entwich, nicht hinter den Berg, uns die Sonne!
  Ein halb Stündchen noch währts bis zum Geläute der Nacht.» –
Unglückseliger! geh und gehorch! Mein Mädchen erwart ich.
  Tröste mich, Lämpchen, indes, lieblicher Bote der Nacht!

XX

Zieret Stärke den Mann und freies mutiges Wesen,
  O! so ziemet ihm fast tiefes Geheimnis noch mehr.
Städtebezwingerin du, Verschwiegenheit! Fürstin der Völker!
  Teure Göttin, die mich sicher durchs Leben geführt,
Welches Schicksal erfahr ich! Es löset scherzend die Muse,
  Amor löset, der Schalk, mir den verschlossenen Mund.
Ach, schon wird es so schwer der Könige Schande verbergen!
  Weder die Krone bedeckt, weder ein phrygischer Bund
Midas' verlängertes Ohr: der nächste Diener entdeckt es,
  Und ihm ängstet und drückt gleich das Geheimnis die Brust.
In die Erde vergrüb er es gern, um sich zu erleichtern:
  Doch die Erde verwahrt solche Geheimnisse nicht;

I find I appreciate marble all the better for it,
    and see with a feeling eye, feel with a seeing hand,
compare and contrast. And if she also steals a few
    daylight hours, I'm compensated by the night shift.
We don't only kiss, we have proper conversations.
    When she naps, I'm left with plenty of time to write.
I've even worked on verses while lying curled beside her,
    tapping the beats of my hexameters on to her back
with gentle fingers. In her lovely sleep, she breathes, breathing
    life into a fire that burns on down to the root of my heart.
Eros adjusts the lamp, recalling those occasions
    he did precisely the same for some famous love poets.

XIV

Put on the lamp, would you… *It's not dark,*
    so why waste fuel? Just leave the curtains open,
the sun is behind those flats there, not below the horizon.
    It's half an hour at least before lighting up time.
You little wretch – do as I ask, my girlfriend's coming.
    Comfort me till then, dear lamp, dear evening star.

XX

Strength, courage and openness become a man, yes,
    but more than that, the profoundest sense of privacy.
Discretion – ultimate influencer, people's princess
    and precious goddess – you have guided me this far.
Now what a fate awaits me. The Muse and that urchin Love
    have somehow tricked me into opening my sealed lips.
It's hard enough as it is to keep down royal scandals.
    A crown is as much use as a flat cap to conceal
Midas's long ears: his groom of the stool spots them
    and at once he reacts, the very knowledge constricting his breathing.
If only he could bury it, bring himself some relief,
    but earth is no resting place for such a secret –

Rohre sprießen hervor und rauschen und lispeln im Winde:
Midas! Midas, der Fürst, trägt ein verlängertes Ohr!
Schwerer wird es nun mir, ein schönes Geheimnis zu wahren;
Ach, den Lippen entquillt Fülle des Herzens so leicht!
Keiner Freundin darf ichs vertraun: sie möchte mich schelten;
Keinem Freunde: vielleicht brächte der Freund mir Gefahr.
Mein Entzücken dem Hain, dem schallenden Felsen zu sagen,
Bin ich endlich nicht jung, bin ich nicht einsam genug.
Dir, Hexameter, dir, Pentameter, sei es vertrauet,
Wie sie des Tags mich erfreut, wie sie des Nachts mich beglückt.
Sie, von vielen Männern gesucht, vermeidet die Schlingen,
Die ihr der Kühnere frech, heimlich der Listige legt;
Klug und zierlich schlüpft sie vorbei und kennet die Wege,
Wo sie der Liebste gewiß lauschend begierig empfängt.
Zaudre, Luna, sie kommt! damit sie der Nachbar nicht sehe;
Rausche, Lüftchen, im Laub! niemand vernehme den Tritt.
Und ihr, wachset und blüht, geliebte Lieder, und wieget
Euch im leisesten Hauch lauer und liebender Luft,
Und entdeckt den Quiriten, wie jene Rohre geschwätzig,
Eines glücklichen Paars schönes Geheimnis zuletzt.

NÄHE DES GELIEBTEN

Ich denke dein, wenn mir der Sonne Schimmer
    Vom Meere strahlt;
Ich denke dein, wenn sich des Mondes Flimmer
    In Quellen malt.

Ich sehe dich, wenn auf dem fernen Wege
    Der Staub sich hebt;
In tiefer Nacht, wenn auf dem schmalen Stege
    Der Wandrer bebt.

reeds soon bring it up and prattle the news to the wind:
    Midas, Midas, they whisper, the king has ass's ears!
For me it's tougher still, and mine is the sweetest of secrets.
    So easy for lips to spill what's now brimfull.
No friend can be trusted. A woman might berate me,
    and men – too likely to turn into dangerous rivals.
As for telling the trees or bellowing from clifftops, no,
    I'm too old for that, nor quite so desperate yet.
Instead, I'll confide in you, my hexameter (of sorts) how she
    each day delights me, and enchants me every night.
The focus of many a male gaze, she slips the nets
    audacious trappers set for her, and the subtle lures
of bashful ones. She'll navigate them cleverly, knowing
    her lover – the keen one, the assertive one – is listening out.
Stay there, moon, in case our neighbour should notice her.
    And wind, some rustling foliage please, to conceal her approach.
Then you, my elegies: growing, flourishing, cradled
    and rocked by the lightest breath of warm and loving air,
reveal to the reading world, like those famous gossiping reeds,
    the happy couple at last, their perfectly beautiful secret.

HER NEARNESS

Schubert's setting of this 1795 lyric is unforgettable. The last line encapsulates some of the difficulties in translating German poetry. Usually English is far less polysyllabic, but the spirit that blows through Goethe's five syllables is hard to capture, especially while retaining the rhyme. I decided to make Goethe's long lines even longer, adding in more unstressed syllables for the sake of the music.

I think of you when the sun comes suddenly shimmering
        towards me from the sea.
I think of you when the moon on a stream is glimmering
        in ripples back at me.

I see you whenever something in the distance causes
        dust to rise on a track,
or a walker at a kissing gate briefly pauses
        to scan the midnight black.

Ich höre dich, wenn dort mit dumpfem Rauschen
    Die Welle steigt.
Im stillen Haine geh ich oft zu lauschen,
    Wenn alles schweigt.

Ich bin bei dir, du seist auch noch so ferne,
    Du bist mir nah!
Die Sonne sinkt, bald leuchten mir die Sterne.
    O wärst du da!

DER ZAUBERLEHRLING

Hat der alte Hexenmeister
Sich doch einmal wegbegeben!
Und nun sollen seine Geister
Auch nach meinem Willen leben.
Seine Wort' und Werke
Merkt ich und den Brauch,
Und mit Geistesstärke
Tu ich Wunder auch.

    Walle! walle
    Manche Strecke,
    Daß, zum Zwecke,
    Wasser fließe
    Und mit reichem, vollem Schwalle
    Zu dem Bade sich ergieße.

I hear you as the waves over there start rearing
      with a dull thudding roar.
I'm often listening in a quiet woodland clearing
      and doing nothing more.

I'm with you: despite the miles of separation,
      you still feel near.
The sun's sinking, and now a constellation.
      I wish you could be here.

THE SORCERER'S APPRENTICE

> *Composed in summer, 1797, when Goethe was 'romping about in the world of the ballads' with Schiller. There are various possible sources for the story. The poem is less well known in English – perhaps because so much depends on the perilously shifting metre and rhyme – but regularly quoted still in Germany when anyone takes on a task which gets too much for them. There is something of Browning's* Pied Piper *about it. Goethe's love of performance is evident: he knew how to hold an audience.*

Since at last the mad old druid
says he must go out, my cunning
plan's to prove I too can do it –
bring his spirit helpers running.
Having watched for days
how his magic's done,
now's my chance to raise
wonders of my own.

    Move it, move it!
    Set things going!
    Make a flowing
    stream around you,
    scoop the water, take it, heave it
    in that bath as I command you!

Und nun komm, du alter Besen!
Nimm die schlechten Lumpenhüllen;
Bist schon lange Knecht gewesen:
Nun erfülle meinen Willen!
Auf zwei Beinen stehe,
Oben sei ein Kopf,
Eile nun und gehe
Mit dem Wassertopf!

    Walle! walle
    Manche Strecke,
    Daß, zum Zwecke,
    Wasser fließe
    Und mit reichem, vollem Schwalle
    Zu dem Bade sich ergieße.

Seht, er läuft zum Ufer nieder!
Wahrlich! ist schon an dem Flusse,
Und mit Blitzesschnelle wieder
Ist er hier mit raschem Gusse.
Schon zum zweiten Male!
Wie das Becken schwillt!
Wie sich jede Schale
Voll mit Wasser füllt!

    Stehe! stehe!
    Denn wir haben
    Deiner Gaben
    Vollgemessen! –
    Ach, ich merk es! Wehe! wehe!
    Hab ich doch das Wort vergessen!

Ach das Wort, worauf am Ende
Er das wird, was er gewesen.
Ach, er läuft und bringt behende!

Broomstick – up, it's show time, haul your
glad rags on, so grey and grimy.
Seems you've seen long service, all you're
fit for now is to obey me.
Stand up like a human
with a human face.
Hurry now. I summon
water to this place.

>Move it, move it!
>Set things going!
>Make a flowing
>stream around you,
>scoop the water, take it, heave it
>in that bath as I command you!

Look, he's dashing to the river.
Really. There already. Quickly
back again as keen as ever,
pours the water bathwards slickly.
Down he goes. Amazing
how the bathtub fills,
how the level's risen
almost till it spills.

>Slow it, slow it.
>I'm impressed, so
>take a rest, oh
>gifted lumber.
>All I need to do is know that
>magic word I can't remember.

Word I need to make him finish,
halt this manic pace he's keeping,
bristly goose-step undiminished.

Wärst du doch der alte Besen!
Immer neue Güsse
Bringt er schnell herein.
Ach! und hundert Flüsse
Stürzen auf mich ein.

    Nein, nicht länger
    Kann ich's lassen;
    Will ihn fassen.
    Das ist Tücke!
    Ach! nun wird mir immer bänger!
    Welche Miene! welche Blicke!

O, du Ausgeburt der Hölle!
Soll das ganze Haus ersaufen?
Seh ich über jede Schwelle
Doch schon Wasserströme laufen.
Ein verruchter Besen,
Der nicht hören will!
Stock, der du gewesen,
Steh doch einmal still!

    Willsts am Ende
    Gar nicht lassen?
    Will dich fassen,
    Will dich halten,
    Und das alte Holz behende
    Mit dem scharfen Beile spalten.

Seht, da kommt er schleppend wieder!
Wie ich mich nun auf dich werfe,
Gleich, o Kobold, liegst du nieder;
Krachend trifft die glatte Schärfe.
Wahrlich! brav getroffen!
Seht, er ist entzwei!
Und nun kann ich hoffen,
Und ich atme frei!

Broom, go back to simple sweeping!
Jugfuls he produces.
Nothing done by halves.
Oh, a hundred sluices
slosh around my calves.

    Stop the show, please,
    can't endure it.
    I'll make sure it –
    ow, that's hopeless.
    Suddenly the scene unnerves me.
    What a glare this broomstick serves me!

Ah, you spawn of all the devils,
do you plan to drown this building?
Everywhere the water level's
rising, doors are barely holding,
rivers of it, cursèd
broom who's playing deaf.
Stick! be what you first were.
Stop, be still, enough!

    Even now you
    can't relax it.
    Here's the exit.
    Hah, I'll show you!
    Split this ancient wood to matches
    with this newly sharpened hatchet.

Look, he's traipsing back towards me.
Soon you won't know quite what hit you.
Knock you flat, hobgoblin, watch me.
Crack, the shiny blade has split you.
Done. And done quite neatly.
Look, he's chopped in two.
Touch wood, I'm completely
finished with this show.

Wehe! Wehe!
Beide Teile
Stehn in Eile
Schon als Knechte
Völlig fertig in die Höhe!
Helft mir, ach! ihr hohen Mächte!

Und sie laufen! Naß und nässer
Wirds im Saal und auf den Stufen.
Welch entsetzliches Gewässer!
Herr und Meister! hör mich rufen! –
Ach, da kommt der Meister!
Herr, die Not ist groß!
Die ich rief, als Geister
Werd ich nun nicht los.

«In die Ecke,
Besen! Besen!
Seids gewesen.
Denn als Geister
Ruft euch nur, zu diesem Zwecke,
Erst hervor der alte Meister.»

FAUST IM STUDIERZIMMER

Habe nun, ach! Philosophie,
Juristerei und Medizin,
Und leider auch Theologie
Durchaus studiert, mit heißem Bemühn.
Da steh ich nun, ich armer Tor,

No, oh no, oh
both the splinters
stand and no, oh
two more sprinters
jugging up and down for hours.
Help me oh you mighty powers!

Back and forth. An inundation.
Hallway, staircase, faster, faster.
What a washed-out revolution.
Guide me, teach me, Lord and master.
Ah, alack, he's here – it's
needed, sir, your knack.
Having called these spirits,
help me send them back…

> *To the corner,*
> *Broom, for ever,*
> *Broom, and never*
> *Will such forces*
> *Work for you or him, I warn you.*
> *Mine they are. Your sorcerer's.*

FAUST IN HIS STUDY

> *This well-known speech comes from* Faust, Part One, *the equivalent of the opening soliloquy in Marlowe's* Doctor Faustus. *Whereas blank verse does the heavy lifting in Renaissance drama, Goethe keeps it light, always looking for variety. Even the rhyme scheme here becomes fascinatingly unreliable.* Faust *is as much a poem as a play.*

So, having read Philosophy
and Medicine and Law and run
the whole length of Theology
in hot pursuit of truth (such fun!)
I stand here now, my IQ score

Und bin so klug als wie zuvor!
Heiße Magister, heiße Doktor gar,
Und ziehe schon an die zehen Jahr
Herauf, herab und quer und krumm
Meine Schüler an der Nase herum –
Und sehe, daß wir nichts wissen können!
Das will mir schier das Herz verbrennen.
Zwar bin ich gescheiter als alle die Laffen,
Doktoren, Magister, Schreiber und Pfaffen;
Mich plagen keine Skrupel noch Zweifel,
Fürchte mich weder vor Hölle noch Teufel –
Dafür ist mir auch alle Freud entrissen,
Bilde mir nicht ein, was Rechts zu wissen,
Bilde mir nicht ein, ich könnte was lehren,
Die Menschen zu bessern und zu bekehren.
Auch hab ich weder Gut noch Geld,
Noch Ehr und Herrlichkeit der Welt:
Es möchte kein Hund so länger leben!
Drum hab ich mich der Magie ergeben,
Ob mir durch Geistes Kraft und Mund
Nicht manch Geheimnis würde kund,
Daß ich nicht mehr mit sauerm Schweiß
Zu sagen brauche, was ich nicht weiß,
Daß ich erkenne, was die Welt
Im Innersten zusammenhält,
Schau alle Wirkenskraft und Samen,
Und tu nicht mehr in Worten kramen.

O sähst du, voller Mondenschein,
Zum letztenmal auf meine Pein,
Den ich so manche Mitternacht
An diesem Pult herangewacht:
Dann über Büchern und Papier,
Trübselger Freund, erschienst du mir!
Ach! könnt ich doch auf Bergeshöhn
In deinem lieben Lichte gehn,
Um Bergeshöhle mit Geistern schweben,
Auf Wiesen in deinem Dämmer weben,
Von allem Wissensqualm entladen,
In deinem Tau gesund mich baden!

exactly what it was before.
An M.A. and a Doctorate
have kept my students aiming at
those marshlights, up and round and back
ten years or more. But here's the fact.
I can confirm for certain we
know nothing – and that tortures me.
It's true I'm better off at least
than those other dons, that do-good priest,
not plagued by vague morality.
Damnation doesn't bother me.
That's why perhaps the fun stopped flowing.
My faith in what I thought worth knowing
or what I felt worth teaching's gone.
My life won't help the world move on.
I have no wealth, no property,
no fame. The world just laughs at me.
A dog's life, only worse. Quite tragic.
And so I've turned at last to magic
to see if spirits can provide
the answers to those things I've tried
bluffing with pedagogic drone,
dodging truths we've never known.
I'll find out from the source the way
our world deep down is run, and see
just how its forces all cohere…
instead of this verbal diarrhoea.

I'm sure you've had your fill, full moon,
of my misfortunes. Sitting alone
with you, those piteous midnight looks
would cross my heaps of scripts and books.
I'd like to walk up mountain paths
by your sweet light, through drifting wraiths
round mountain caves. I'd like to linger
on meadows and to feel no longer
burdened by intellect, but free
to bathe in your healing poetry.

Weh! steck ich in dem Kerker noch?
Verfluchtes dumpfes Mauerloch,
Wo selbst das liebe Himmelslicht
Trüb durch gemalte Scheiben bricht!
Beschränkt von diesem Bücherhauf,
Den Würme nagen, Staub bedeckt,
Den bis ans hohe Gewölb hinauf
Ein angeraucht Papier umsteckt;
Mit Gläsern, Büchsen rings umstellt,
Mit Instrumenten vollgepfropft,
Urväterhausrat drein gestopft –
Das ist deine Welt! das heißt eine Welt!

Und fragst du noch, warum dein Herz
Sich bang in deinem Busen klemmt?
Warum ein unerklärter Schmerz
Dir alle Lebensregung hemmt?
Statt der lebendigen Natur,
Da Gott die Menschen schuf hinein,
Umgibt in Rauch und Moder nur
Dich Tiergeripp und Totenbein!
Flieh! auf! hinaus ins weite Land!
Und dies geheimnisvolle Buch,
Von Nostradamus' eigner Hand,
Ist dir es nicht Geleit genug?
Erkennest dann der Sterne Lauf,
Und wenn Natur dich unterweist,
Dann geht die Seelenkraft dir auf,
Wie spricht ein Geist zum andern Geist.
Umsonst, daß trocknes Sinnen hier
Die heilgen Zeichen dir erklärt!
Ihr schwebt, ihr Geister, neben mir:
Antwortet mir, wenn ihr mich hört!

But no, I'm in this dungeon still,
this wretched dank unwholesome cell
where even the blessed light of day
finds murky stained glass in its way.
Imprisoned with these heaped up tomes,
the smoke-discoloured paper peeling,
encased in dust and gnawed by worms,
right up into the vaulted ceiling,
with apparatus ages old
in scattered random piles, all sorts
of beakers, tubes and glass retorts –
that's your world, Faust. And what a world!

Yet still you keep on asking why
you feel this numb and nameless ache,
a pressure in your heart so high
it holds all your ambition back.
Instead of nature's living breath
designed by kindly providence,
you breathe in mould and motes of death:
stuffed animals and skeletons.
Get up, then. Find a world outside.
But take these texts in holograph
by Nostradamus for your guide:
he'll tell you how the stars can move
across that far occult horizon,
he'll show you (now that nature's sworn
accomplice to your soul) those rising
ghosts as they call like birds at dawn.
Why go on searching pointlessly
for holy truth in a dry well
when spirits are hovering next to me?
Let's hear what secrets they can tell…

NATUR UND KUNST

Natur und Kunst, sie scheinen sich zu fliehen,
Und haben sich, eh man es denkt, gefunden;
Der Widerwille ist auch mir verschwunden,
Und beide scheinen gleich mich anzuziehen.

Es gilt wohl nur ein redliches Bemühen!
Und wenn wir erst in abgemeßnen Stunden
Mit Geist und Fleiß uns an die Kunst gebunden,
Mag frei Natur im Herzen wieder glühen.

So ists mit aller Bildung auch beschaffen:
Vergebens werden ungebundne Geister
Nach der Vollendung reiner Höhe streben.

Wer Großes will, muß sich zusammenraffen;
In der Beschränkung zeigt sich erst der Meister,
Und das Gesetz nur kann uns Freiheit geben.

NATURE AND ART

> *Whereas eighteenth-century writers shunned the sonnet, it became a hallmark of the Romantics. Goethe bestrides the two eras, and turned to the sonnet at the start of the nineteenth century. He wrote a cycle in 1807 following affairs with Minna Herzlieb and Silvie von Ziegesar. This one was written in 1800 and published in 1809.*

Though art and nature can seem poles apart,
they come together soon enough, their wars
forgotten; and my own resistance tires.
I sense the power that both of them exert.

It's just a case of working long and late.
So once we've spent, let's say, ten thousand hours
on steering, footwork, shifting through the gears,
it may be then some natural move feels right.

Creative though you be, you'll strive in vain
to reach perfection if you've no technique,
however wired and woke your gifts may be.

You want a masterpiece? You'll need to strain
those sinews, set your limits, drill and hack.
The rules are all we have to set us free.

BIOGRAPHICAL NOTES

JOHANN WOLFGANG VON GOETHE was born in Frankfurt-on-Main in 1749 and studied law at Leipzig (where he was more interested in the occult – alchemy fascinated him – and then Strasbourg, where Herder's influence was crucial,[1] and led him to Shakespeare.

From a young age Goethe was prolific as a poet, his first collection appearing when he was twenty. Some of his best known, most impassioned lyrics are from his youth. Plays too attracted him early on – he was given a puppet theatre for Christmas when he was four – and it was the play *Götz von Berlichingen* which brought his first national success (Sir Walter Scott translated it). More overwhelming was the impact of his novella the following year: *The Sorrows of Young Werther* (1774, revised 1787), with its controversial suicide, was to influence a generation. Invited to the Court of Weimar in 1775, Goethe made it the centre of his subsequent operations and wrote many major works there, including *Egmont* (for which Beethoven wrote his overture) and the autobiographical novel *Wilhelm Meister*.

But he was a restless man, whose travels and relationships fed especially into his poetry – there is enough to fill 1500 pages, much of it from later years when he composed the immense *West-Eastern Divan*. His travels to Italy (described in *The Italian Journey*) fostered a classical period, prompting the plays *Iphigenia in Tauris* and *Torquato Tasso* and some extensive verse sequences. During the year 1797/8 he wrote the epic *Hermann and Dorothea* and his celebrated ballads, at much the same time as Wordsworth and Coleridge were publishing theirs. Like Coleridge, Goethe loved conversation and among his many friendships Schiller's was most

---

[1] Johann Gottfried Herder was a German philosopher, theologian, poet, and literary critic. He is associated with the Enlightenment, *Sturm und Drang*, and Weimar Classicism.

important, particularly helping him understand drama. The complexities of his relationships with women are harder to untangle although *Werther* and the novel *Elective Affinities* give us some idea. Suffice to say that his engagement to Lili Schönemann was broken off before he moved to Weimar, he had an enduring bond with the playwright Charlotte von Stein and a long partnership, children and eventual marriage with Christiane Vulpius. Goethe worked on his dramatic poem, *Faust*, for much of his creative life and the first of its two parts is considered his masterpiece.

Although best known as a man of letters, translator, editor, playwright and poet, he was active in public affairs as an administrator and a soldier – the archetypal polymath. Indeed, Goethe's scientific researches into optics, colour ('Farbenlehre') and the 'metamorphosis of plants' are only now being fully appreciated.

He died on 22nd March, 1832.

JOHN GREENING (b. 1954) has published over twenty collections, notably *To the War Poets* (2013) and *The Silence* (2019), both with Carcanet. There have been several recent pamphlets and his selected reviews and essays on poetry (*Vapour Trails*) appeared in 2020. Earlier books include *Heath*, with Penelope Shuttle and the Egypt memoir, *Threading a Dream*.

He has edited Edmund Blunden's *Undertones of War* for Oxford and the poetry of Geoffrey Grigson and Iain Crichton Smith (Carcanet, 2021). His critical studies cover the Elizabethans, Hardy, Yeats, Edward Thomas, WW1 Poets, and Ted Hughes. Anthologies include *Accompanied Voices: Poets on Composers* and *Hollow Palaces* (modern country house poems – with Kevin Gardner, Liverpool UP, 2021). Dr. Gardner has also edited a selection of Greening's poetry for American readers, *The Interpretation of Owls: Poems 1977-2022*, which appears from Baylor University Press in 2023.

A longstanding *TLS* reviewer and Gregory Award judge, John Greening has collaborated with musicians such as Roderick Williams, Cecilia McDowall and Philip Lancaster. He has received the Bridport Prize, the *TLS* Prize, an Arvon and a Cholmondeley Award, and was until recently Royal Literary Fund Writing Fellow at Newnham College, Cambridge.